SALLON'S
WAR

SALLON'S
WAR

RALPH SALLON

Foreword by
MICHAEL FOOT

Introduction by
MARTIN GILBERT

Sponsored by
THE DAILY MIRROR

ANDRE DEUTSCH

First published in Great Britain in 1994 by
André Deutsch Limited
106 Great Russell Street
London WC1B 3LJ

ISBN 0 233 98909 9

Cataloguing-in-Publication data available for this title from
the British Library

Printed in Great Britain by
St Edmundsbury Press, Bury St Edmunds, Suffolk

FOREWORD
Michael Foot

Thomas Carlyle insisted on having a portrait of his heroes or villains, there on his desk or mantelpiece, when he wrote about them. He would never miss some aspect of their character which others might overlook. I remember the portrait of Mazzini, Carlyle's own, which my father kept on his mantelpiece. No one thereafter in our household could vilify the great Mazzini, as some historians tended to do.

Carlyle, a wonderful portrait painter in words, would, I am sure, have appreciated Sallon's work. He can caricature or vilify when he wishes. Plenty of his Second World War characters deserve nothing else, and they get it. His whole range is extraordinary, but for me, anyhow, the best are the sympathetic ones: say, his Albert Einstein of 1934 or his H G Wells of just about the same period which hangs on my wall, as I seek to write about him. I know there are several other H G's, but this is the friendly master of Cockney humour I love best.

I first met Sallon myself in the 1940s when I joined the *Daily Herald* as a columnist. He helped to teach us all what that war was about and how we should work for a better peace at the end: the kind which Einstein and Wells had campaigned for all their lives. I am so glad to see his portraits properly reprinted.

April 1994

INTRODUCTION
by Martin Gilbert

A meeting with Ralph Sallon when he was already in his nineties was my first introduction to his wit and humanity. It was James Cameron who wrote: 'All satirists cause pain, because they traffic in the rasping medium of truth', and there is certainly something painful, both for his character and his nation, in the Neville Chamberlain drawing which Sallon did at the time of the Munich crisis in 1938. But there is also an amazing breadth of kindness and fun in Sallon's drawings, which span more than four decades and which introduce us, as they introduced newspaper readers over many years, to the characters, and characteristics, of a bygone age.

Sallon was born in 1899, in one of the provinces of Russian Poland, in the village of Sheps, near Warsaw. It was a time when Jewish families such as his own faced many dilemmas and hardships, not least the constant danger of anti-Semitic attack, discrimination at school and university, financial privation and the constant fear besetting a minority that was made to feel alien both by its Russian masters and its Polish fellow-subjects.

Leaving the land and regime of the Tsar, the Sallons made their way, as did tens of thousands of other Jews, to Britain. Ralph Sallon was four years old when his parents reached Whitechapel, at that time the hub of Jewish life in London, its tenements and markets awash with the aspirations of newcomers who wanted to make for themselves and their offspring a better life, in every sense of the word, than was possible in the Russian dominions.

In 1914, at the age of fifteen, Sallon won a scholarship to Hornsey Art School but he was only able to study there for a single term, for the scholarship was not enough to enable him to support the many family members who looked to him for their sustenance. He was forced to work in a factory. Later he joined the army. His term at Hornsey proved to be his only formal art training.

After leaving the army in 1921, Sallon went to South Africa, another land that had provided a haven for several generations of Jews fleeing from Tsarist persecution. There he produced his first caricatures, which were published in the *Natal Mercury* in Durban. Soon after he returned to England, where he began to draw, and regularly publish, caricatures and sketches. 'He is bound to go a long way, for his work has already set all London talking,' was the comment of *Everybody's Weekly*. Sallon later summed up his own view of his work in the words: 'Everything is written in the face. Caricature is an inborn peculiarity of vision. For me it is the most fascinating thing in the world.'

For more than twenty years, Sallon's sketches and portraits of the public figures of the time appeared in many newspapers and magazines, including the *Tatler*, the *Bystander, Sporting and Dramatic News* and *Blighty*. Sallon made it his task to track down those whom he wished to draw. In 1925 he had the audacity to call, uninvited, on H.G Wells, at his flat in Whitehall. A sleepy but bemused 'H.G.' (who could also be irascible) invited him in and, while he was cooking breakfast, allowed Sallon to portray him in bedroom slippers and dressing gown.

At a banquet in 1930, honouring Albert Einstein, the drawing that Sallon did while the meal was in progress was then passed along the table from guest to guest, until it reached the great man. Einstein signed the drawing, which was then passed back to Sallon: it still bears the wine stains of its journey.

Visiting London at that time, for the Round Table Conference on the future of India, was Mahatma Gandhi. Sallon found it difficult to know where to go in order to draw him. Finally, he joined the small crowd outside the Indian High Commission in the Aldwych. 'He hid himself away in there, didn't want anyone to see him,' Sallon later recalled, 'but I found out when he was due to leave and waited for him outside. I drew him as he was crossing the road.'

Sallon made sure that he was in the right place at the right time, as far as catching the good and the great was concerned. In the foyer of Claridges Hotel, in the early 1930s, he espied Queen Astrid of the Belgians, wife of King Leopold. 'She was one of the most beautiful women I ever sketched,' Sallon later commented. When a slightly inebriated Prince of Wales (later Duke of Windsor) passed by on his way to call on the King and Queen, he looked at the sketch and then murmured in the artist's ear, 'Good heavens Sallon, she won't like that, she won't like that at all.'

In 1934, Sallon returned for a short visit to his birthplace, formerly part of the Russian Empire, then (and now) in Poland. Accompanied by his mother, he visited his many relations who still lived there. Almost all of them were later murdered during the Holocaust. While he was in Warsaw, Sallon saw the Polish First World War hero and national leader, Marshal Pilsudski, in a procession and drew him as he passed by.

At a State banquet for Joachim von Ribbentrop, Hitler's Ambassador to Britain, Sallon sketched the man who was to be Foreign Minister of the Third Reich from 1938 until 1945. When asked if he had shown Ribbentrop the sketch he replied, 'No, I didn't show him the drawing, you can never make tyrants laugh.'

One of those who were at the centre of the appeasement controversy was Sir Nevile Henderson, the British Ambassador in Berlin at the time of the Munich crisis. Sallon commented on his drawing of Henderson: 'He reminded me of Hitler to look at, so I drew Hitler on the bottom of the drawing.' When war came in 1939, Sallon was one of those on Hitler's blacklist of people to be arrested as soon as Britain was defeated. So too was Sallon's fellow cartoonist, the New Zealander David Low.

During the Second World War, Sallon joined the *Daily Mail* and later worked on the Labour *Daily Herald*. His drawings of the Nazi leaders captured those evil impulses that had led them to war and to the persecution of Sallon's own people. He also worked for a clandestine Belgian newspaper that was dropped into that German-occupied country: there, his Goebbels ('I drew him breathing fire'), Goering and Himmler were hated figures, and the motto 'Laughter is the great enemy of tyranny' was an inspiration to him and a beacon to the captive peoples. Today, a set of them is housed, and honoured, at the National Art Museum in Antwerp.

After the war Sallon joined the permanent staff of the *Daily Mirror*, drawing for the paper for the next forty years. He was also commissioned by Butterworths, the legal publishers, to produce a 'Legal Series' of twelve Lord Chief Justices, the first such series since that done by Sallon's Victorian predecessor, Spy.

Many of Sallon's drawings were done at the Press Club or at press conferences, where he was a familiar figure with his pencils and small sketch pads. One such press conference was for Humphrey Bogart and Lauren Bacall. 'There was a huge crowd around them,' Sallon later recalled. 'I heard them whistling to each other, just so they knew where the other one was.'

Sallon drew many actors, conductors and singers. Backstage,

after the pantomime *Peter Pan* was over, he drew the actor Donald Wolfit. During a cabaret performance at the Dorchester Hotel in the 1960s he drew Marlene Dietrich. Of the comedian Arthur Askey, whom he sketched, he later recalled: 'We both had the same outlook, to make people laugh. In between his jokes he always gave a little dance. That's how I drew him.'

Commenting on his own work, Sallon said: 'I am not interested in whether people like my drawings, I am only interested in telling the truth. My drawings, by slightly exaggerating the essential points, make people look more like themselves than they are.' As to the politicans, who were his staple fare: 'They all like to be drawn. The only way to insult them is *not* to draw them.'

In 1979, Sallon was awarded the MBE. At a reception in the Press Club, Lord Hailsham, whom he had first sketched forty years earlier, remarked: 'Sallon is the doyen of caricaturists today.' He was still drawing a decade later.

May 1994

NEVILLE CHAMBERLAIN

British Prime Minister, 1937–40

WINSTON CHURCHILL

British Prime Minister, 1940–45 and 1951–55

WINSTON CHURCHILL

FIELD MARSHAL VISCOUNT MONTGOMERY

Commander of the 21st Army Group from
Normandy to the Rhine and into Germany

GENERAL DE GAULLE

CHARLES DE GAULLE

Leader of the Free French movement, 1940–45
and President of France, 1959–69

LÉON BLUM

Head of the Popular Front in France in 1936
and later French Prime Minister, 1936–37, 1938 and 1946–47

MARSHAL HENRI-PHILIPPE PÉTAIN

Supporter of the armistice with Germany in 1940 and Head of
State of Vichy France. Sentenced to life imprisonment in 1945

PIERRE LAVAL

Twice Prime Minister of France between the wars and
Prime Minister of Vichy France, 1942–44

EDOUARD DALADIER

French Prime Minister at the time of the Munich Agreement, arrested by
Vichy authorities and interned by the Germans after the fall of France

JOSEPH STALIN

Soviet dictator from the mid-1920s until his death in 1953

ADOLF HITLER

Founder and leader of the Nazi Party and German dictator, 1933–45

HERMANN GOERING

Founder of the Gestapo, set up the first concentration camps
and Head of the German Air Force, 1935

DR JOSEF GOEBBELS

Head of the Ministry of Public Enlightenment and Propaganda
for the Nazi Party, 1933–45

RUDOLF HESS

Hitler's deputy, sentenced to life imprisonment in Spandau
Prison at the Nuremberg Trials

HEINRICH HIMMLER

Hitler follower and an initiator of the mass murder of the Jews

GRAND-ADMIRAL DOENITZ

Head of Germany's U-Boat campaign from
1939 and brief ruler of the Third Reich
following Hitler's suicide

FIELD MARSHAL VON RUNDSTEDT

Directed the German attack on Poland in 1939
and on France in 1940

GENERAL ERWIN ROMMEL

Known as 'The Desert Fox', Britain's main military adversary
in North Africa and Normandy

JOACHIM VON RIBBENTROP

Hitler's Ambassador to Britain in 1936 and German Foreign Minister, 1938–45

KING UMBERTO OF ITALY

Forced to abdicate in 1946, his first year as king, when Italy
became a republic and lived in exile in Portugal until his death in 1983

JAN MASARYK

Czech Ambassador to London, 1938 and
Foreign Minister during and immediately after
World War II

EDUARD BENĚS

Czech President, 1935–38 and 1945–48

MARSHAL PILSUDSKI

Head of State and Commander-in-Chief of the new Polish
Republic in 1919 and Polish Prime Minister and Minister of war,
1926–27

GENERAL SIKORSKI

Polish statesman

KING HAAKON OF NORWAY

Became king in 1905 but fled the country after the German invasion in 1940. Returned in 1945 and reigned until his death in 1957

QUEEN ASTRID OF THE BELGIANS

KING GEORGE OF GREECE

MARSHAL TITO

Leader of the communist partisans in Yugoslavia during World
War II and Prime Minister of Yugoslavia from 1945–53 and
President from 1953 until his death in 1980

PRINCE PAUL OF YUGOSLAVIA

Regent of Yugoslavia for his nephew Peter,
overthrown in 1941

PRINCE PETER OF YUGOSLAVIA

KING PETER OF YUGOSLAVIA

GENERALISSIMO FRANCISCO FRANCO

Spanish dictator following his leadership of the
Nationalist forces in the Spanish Civil War

THE DUKE OF ALBA

Spanish Ambassador in London during World War II

CHIANG KAI-SHEK

Head of the Chinese Nationalist Republic, 1928–49

HIROHITO

Emperor of Japan, 1926–89

PU YI

The last Chinese Emperor

HAILE SELASSE

Emperor of Abyssinia. Fled the country after the Italian invasion in 1936,
returned as Emperor after the British liberation in 1941

MAHATMA GANDHI

Indian Nationalist leader who led the country
to Independence in 1947

EAMON DE VALERA

Irish Nationalist leader and Prime Minister of the Irish Free
State, 1932–48, 1951–54 and 1957–59. President of Ireland,
1959–73

SIR STAFFORD CRIPPS

Churchill's Ambassador to Moscow, 1940–42,
later Chancellor of the Exchequer in the 1945 Labour Government

ERNEST BEVIN

Minister of Labour in Churchill's all-party War Cabinet,
later Foreign Secretary in the first post-war Labour
Government

HERBERT MORRISON

Churchill's Home Secretary, 1940–45 and Deputy Prime
Minister in the 1945 Labour Government

ANEURIN BEVAN

Labour politician and Minister of Health, 1945–51

THE EARL OF SWINTON

Secretary of State for Air

VISCOUNT CRANBORNE
(LATER MARQUESS OF SALISBURY)

Secretary of State for the Dominions during World War II

GENERAL SIR HASTINGS ISMAY
(LATER LORD ISMAY)

Head of Churchill's Defence Office during
World War II

ALFRED DUFF COOPER

First Lord of the Admiralty in 1938

LEO AMERY

Secretary of State for India

SIR HARTLEY SHAWCROSS

Lawyer and Chief United Kingdom
prosecutor at the Nuremberg Trials

SIR NEVILE HENDERSON

British Ambassador to Berlin, 1937 until the
outbreak of World War II

WILLIAM BEVERIDGE

Author of the Beveridge Report, advocating
widespread State-financed social services,
including a National Health Service

SIR ARCHIBALD MCINDOE

New Zealand plastic surgeon whose pioneering work
rehabilitated hundreds of Battle of Britain pilots

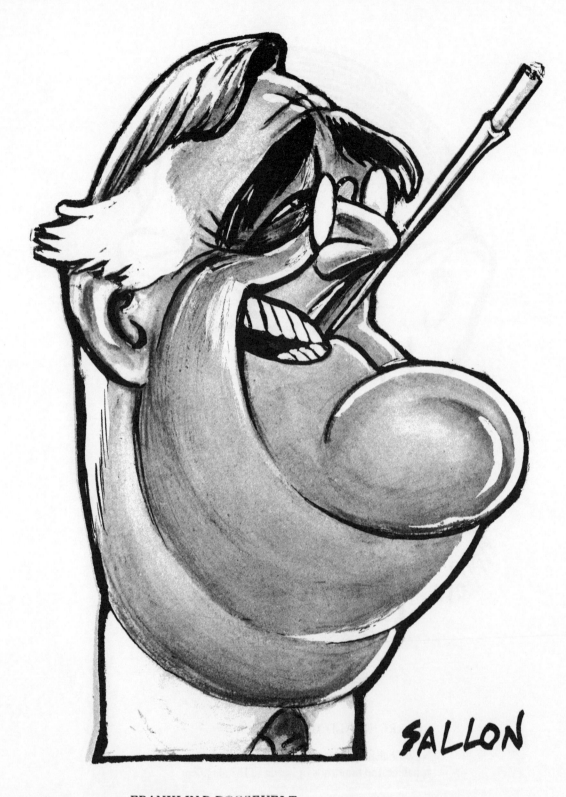

SALLON

FRANKLIN D ROOSEVELT

President of the United States, 1933–45 and launched the New
Deal to end the Depression

ELEANOR ROOSEVELT
First Lady of the United States, 1933–45 and active social reformer

GENERAL DWIGHT D EISENHOWER

President of the United States, 1953–61

GENERAL GEORGE S PATTON

Military commander and leading exponent of
mobile tank warfare

GENERAL SIMPSON

American general during World War II

GENERAL GEORGE C MARSHALL

Chief of Staff of the United States Army, 1939–45

GENERAL OMAR N BRADLEY

Military commander of the United States 1st Army, 1944

HARRY S TRUMAN
President of the United States following Roosevelt's death,
authorised the dropping of the atom bomb in Hiroshima (1945)

MARLENE DIETRICH

Film and cabaret star

JOSEPHINE BAKER

Dancer

LAUREN BACALL

Film actress

HUMPHREY BOGART

Film actor

SIR DONALD WOLFIT

Actor

ARTHUR ASKEY

Comedian

BUD FLANAGAN

Comedian

SIR RALPH VAUGHAN WILLIAMS

Composer

SIR HENRY WOOD

Conductor

HENRY HALL

Conductor

BERTRAND RUSSELL

Philosopher, mathematician and pacifist

ALBERT EINSTEIN

German physicist and proponent of the Theory of Relativity

GEORGE BERNARD SHAW

Dramatist, literary critic and active Socialist

Sketch
to
H G Wells

H G WELLS

Writer of novels and science fiction

J B PRIESTLEY

Novelist, playwright and essayist

GRAHAM GREENE

Novelist and short story writer

ILYA EHRENBURG

Soviet writer

AVERELL HARRIMAN

American politician and diplomat

GENERAL CHARLES G DAWES

American banker

GORDON SELFRIDGE

Sketched outside Selfridges Department Store
during the London Blitz

KATE

A cart minder